RUN, LIF

MW00464149

Volume 1

12 Obstacle Course Racing Workouts That Took Us to the World Championships

By

Riley Nadoroznick

ISBN: 9781520682839

TrainWithConviction.com

CONVICTION

STRENGTH - ENDURANCE - LIFESTYLE

www.TrainWithConviction.com

Dedication

To my Conviction Fitness family. This book, and our team, would be nothing without you.

"No matter your level of experience, training with a team accelerates your development."

- **Former Navy SEAL Commander Mark Divine**

Disclaimer

This book does not contain medical guidelines but is for educational and entertainment purposes only.

You must consult your physician prior to starting this program or if you have any medical condition or injury that contradicts physical activity. This program is designed for healthy individuals 18 years and older only.

The information in this book is not meant to supplement, nor replace, proper exercise training. All forms of exercise pose some inherent risks. The author advises readers to take full responsibility for their safety and know their limits.

Before each workout be sure that your equipment is well-maintained and do not take risks beyond your level of experience, aptitude, training, or fitness. The exercises and dietary programs in this book are not intended as a substitute for any exercise routine or treatment or dietary regimen that may have been prescribed by your physician. Again, you must check with your physician before starting this program.

Do not lift weights if you are alone, inexperienced, injured, or fatigued. Always ask for instruction and assistance when lifting. Never perform any exercise without proper instruction.

If you are taking any medications, you must talk to your physician before starting this exercise program.

Have fun.

TABLE OF CONTENTS

INTRODUCTION

I am not a World Champion.

I don't know what it's like to have big sponsorships. I don't get free equipment or flown in to races. I've never even run a half-marathon and my fastest 5k is barely sub 20:00.

I am far from what I would call a great Obstacle Course Racer. But I love this sport and I've dedicated a large part of my life to it over the past three years.

I'm just a regular guy. A happily married father of four, a strength and conditioning coach, and a business owner.

I consider myself the luckiest guy in the world. I have the most amazing family anyone could ask for and spend my days helping others reach their health, fitness, and – more specifically, Obstacle Course Racing (OCR) goals.

Our team at Conviction Fitness is very close, and my athletes have become a second family to me.

While spending my entire day out on the trails without a care in the world does sound appealing sometimes, that's just not who I am.

Between running a business, coaching other athletes, helping my kids with homework, and taking them to their activities, I don't have much more than 7 or 8 hours per week to train.

And that's pushing it sometimes.

Most of the athletes I coach are in a similar situation. They have families, pets, and busy professional lives. They sit on volunteer boards and take time to give back to their community.

There's always something going on in our lives, but we never let training fall to the wayside. We're always sure to make time to train for and compete in this wonderful sport of OCR.

Our lives aren't overly conducive to becoming great endurance athletes. Because of this, we need to train differently than most - much different than the pros.

If you have unlimited time for training and choose to spend most your life doing so, then this probably isn't the book for you.

But if you, like us, live busy lives outside of OCR, I believe the fun and time-efficient workouts you're about to discover can help you.

Through our training – through the exact workouts described in this book – my teammates and I have achieved more than we ever thought possible.

We don't spend ours a day training. We don't use fancy equipment. We don't have access to state-of-the-art recovery systems and methods, yet we've transformed ourselves from half-decent Open category athletes into top-10 finishing Spartan Elites.

We've raced in internationally televised events, and competed on the world stage.

In 2016, over 70% of all our athletes qualified for the OCR World Championships, while 80% of our Elite Spartan Racers qualified for the Spartan Race World Championships.

Two of our Competitive Division Spartan Racers, Matt Yarnton, and Ara Steininger, finished the season ranked 3rd and 10th overall in all of Canada.

Not bad, if you ask me.

We enjoy our training, but it doesn't consume our entire lives. Our workouts are short, intense, and effective.

You likely won't win the World Championships simply following the workouts in this book. But that's not the goal here.

What I believe this book will do for you is help you fall in love with your training, and become a faster, more confident obstacle course racer.

We proved that it's possible to go far in OCR without devoting your entire life to training.

Now it's your turn.

OUTLINE

This is simple book contains 12 different workouts we've used in our Spartan SGX training program at Conviction Fitness.

These are the exact workouts we relied on to help our athletes qualify for both the Spartan Race World Championships and Obstacle Course Racing World Championships in 2016.

The workouts are broken up into four different categories:

- Hill Workouts
- Interval Workouts
- AMRAP Workouts
- For Time Workouts

Not only does this variety of training methods make us better athletes, but it also helps to keep things fresh in our training. No one wants to do the same old routine over and over.

Each category of workout contains three separate training sessions, and most training sessions have at least one sample four-week progression.

If you take each workout progression into consideration, there are technically over 50 different workouts in this book.

After introducing you to the movements we use, we'll walk you through each workout and its progressions.

The Overload Principle – Why We Use Progressions

If you were to take a personal trainer or fitness coach certification, one of the topics covered would undoubtedly be the Overload Principle.

What this principle states, essentially, is that to continuously improve we must work progressively harder as our bodies adjust to our existing workouts.

Doing three sets of 20 push-ups three days a week, for example, will only take you so far. If you want to continue to improve, you need to work harder.

This can mean a few different things. Increasing reps, adding sets, shortening rest periods, using slightly harder exercises (e.g. close-grip push-ups in the above example), and adding resistance (e.g. weighted or banded push-ups) are all great ways to "make things harder".

We provide examples and recommendations for progressing each of the 12 workouts in this book.

At the end of this book, you'll find three different examples of how to incorporate these workouts into your training – based on a two, three, or four days a week training plan.

If you're looking to add some fun and excitement to your training and become a better obstacle course racer in the process, then read on.

Happy training!

Required Equipment

We run a lean operation.

You won't find preacher curl stations, pec decks, or even treadmills where we train. We prefer basic, bare bones training. The type of training you can do anywhere, anytime.

Kettlebells, pull-ups bars, gymnastics rings, sandbags, and buckets are all you'll find in our gym. And when we're outdoors, we make use of our surroundings – hills, rocks, trees, and trails allow us to train while breathing in the fresh air.

To properly do all the workouts listed in this book, all you need is somewhere to do pull-ups and a heavy object of some sort (kettlebell, barbell, sandbag, rock… whatever you prefer).

While a workout may suggest using a sandbag or a kettlebell, feel free to try different things.

9

Don't have a pair of kettlebells for farmer walks? Grab a couple of cinder blocks and carry those.

Don't want to take your sandbag camping? No problem, find a large rock and get some work in.

Never let a lack of equipment stop you from training.

Enter the Courage Corner

In his book, "The Russian Kettlebell Challenge", Pavel Tsatsouline, introduced us to the idea of a "Courage Corner". He wrote:

"The Red Army, too pragmatic to waste their troopers' time on pushups and sit-ups, quickly caught on. Every Russian military unit, even outposts remote as the planet Mars, has a gym. For some strange reason, maybe because it makes your sweaty basement dungeon look like a yuppie health spa, it is called a 'courage corner' (I wish it was a joke). Every courage corner, including the permafrost-crusted cave in one of the units I served in, is equipped with K-bells."

These "Courage Corners" employed by the Russian Army were far from fancy health clubs - a few kettlebells and just enough space to use them is all you'd find. Yet, the strength and conditioning these soldiers developed made them the envy of other countries.

Even without all the expensive equipment seen in most gyms today, these soldiers turned themselves into strong, powerful, athletic beasts.

An obstacle course racer with trails to run on and a Courage Corner to lift in is an obstacle racer set-up for success.

THE MOVEMENTS

There are several different movements that make up the workouts described in this book. While most of these will be familiar to you, it never hurts to have a little refresher.

These movements can be done any time, any place.

When it comes time to start doing the workouts listed in this book, I would suggest changing where you train on a regular basis. Not only will this help to keep things fresh, but it also provides an opportunity to get out and explore your surroundings. You never know what hidden gem you might find.

The following is a brief description of how to properly execute each movement referred to in our workouts.

Remember, good form is the key to longevity and success. It doesn't matter how many burpees or swings you do if you're doing them wrong.

And it doesn't matter how fast you are if you're sitting on the sideline come race day.

BURPEE

Start from a standing position.

Drop down into a plank.

Do a complete push-up, chest touching the ground.

Push yourself back up, hop your feet in and stand up.
Finish by jumping off the ground, lifting your hands up
over your head.

Hollow Rock

Lie on your back with arms reaching overhead.

Tighten abs and glutes and form a crescent moon.

Rock back and forth while maintaining this position.

LOADED CARRIES

There are several different variations of loaded carries we use in our training. Sandbag carries, farmer's walks, bucket carries, and all other loaded carry variations are great ways to improve conditioning, work capacity, and mental toughness.

*You want to build **grit**? Loaded carries are the answer.*

Some of our favorite loaded carry variations include:

Sandbag Carry

Sandbag Zercher Carry

Waiter Walk

Front-Rack Walk

Suitcase Carry

Farmer Walk

Bucket Carry

Fireman Carry

Why So Many Loaded Carries?

Not only are loaded carries an actual obstacle at most races, but they are also a great way to strengthen the entire midsection.

Dr. Stuart McGill, a professor of spine biomechanics at the University of Waterloo, has done massive amounts of research on the topic of core function, spine mechanics, and strongman training. His research shows that loaded carries are great exercises for training the abdominal wall, external obliques and quadratus lumborum, creating stability in the trunk.

Bill Hartman, another prominent physical therapist, has also shown how loaded carries can teach us to pull the rib cage down while bracing through the midsection, which improves our posture and places the diaphragm in the proper position.

A stronger core, improved posture, and better breathing (by means of a properly positioned diaphragm) make loaded carries a very important part of our training.

We use several variations of loaded carries to help keep things fresh and avoid overuse injuries.

LUNGE

Begin standing straight up, feet together.

Step out with one leg and kneel to opposite knee.
Make sure both knees are at 90 degrees.

PULL-UP

Grab bar with shoulder width grip. Be sure to mix your grips throughout your training (palms out, in, etc.).

Squeeze the bar and pull yourself up until your chin is above the bar.

Push-Press

Clean the weight up to the front-rack position.

Bend your knees slightly and dip down as you would to perform a vertical jump.

Explode up, pushing the weight and extending your arms all the way over your head.

PUSH-UP

Get in plank position with hands shoulder width and feet together.

Tighten your abs and glutes and lower yourself down until your chest touches the ground.

Push yourself back up.

Swing

Place a kettlebell on the floor in front of you.

Hike the weight back between your legs until your forearms contact your inner thighs.

Explosively thrust your hips forward, launching the bell to chest height. Don't lift with your arms, use your hips! Tighten abs and glutes at the top of each rep.

Let the weight fall back down between your legs, hinging back at the last moment. Do all the reps without setting the weight down.

Alternatives for the Swing?

The kettlebell swing has quickly become one of our favorite movements. There's simply no better option for improving strength, posture, and conditioning with one exercise.

The only downside to the swing is that it requires a kettlebell or dumbbell to execute. While I strongly suggest getting a kettlebell or two for your Courage Corner, I realize they can be expensive.

I'm confident you'd find they are worth the investment should you pick one up, but maybe it just isn't in the budget right now. These races are expensive.

If that's the case, I'd suggest picking up a cinder block from your local hardware store. They range in weight from 35 – 45 lbs., and cost less than $5.

SQUAT

Stand straight with feet about shoulder width apart, toes pointing forward.

Sit back, pushing your knees slightly outward, sitting as low as you can.

Leading with your hips/butt, stand back up.

ZERCHER SQUAT

Stand straight, feet shoulder width apart, toes pointing forward. Sit weight across crook of your arms.

Sit back, pushing your knees slightly outward, sitting as low as you can.

Leading with your hips/butt, stand back up.

Why the Zercher Squat?

We use the Zercher squat in our training for several reasons.

It's easy to learn, it enables you to fully extend your hips at the top (unlike back squats), it works the midsection very intensely (carrying over to loaded carries during a race), and they're easy on the wrists, elbows, and shoulders.

Plus, it's much easier to dump a weight from the Zercher than any other position. When doing squats for time, there is no safer option than the Zercher.

THE WORKOUTS

Hill Workouts

The importance of including hill work should be obvious.

Race directors and course designers are often looking for the toughest terrain to hold their races on, and nine times out of ten, this means rough, hilly terrain.

You can train all you want on a flat surface, but you'll have a hard time running up a 40% grade mountain unless you've dedicated some of your training to climbing.

Not only is hill running a great way to prepare you for the hills you'll find on race day, but it can also make you a stronger, faster, and *healthier* runner in general.

Hill running has been shown to:

- Increase leg strength
- Make your stride longer and quicker
- Enhance running economy; and
- Improve elasticity of muscles, tendons and ligaments

I see far too many coaches and athletes avoiding hills in their training. It doesn't matter if there aren't any hills nearby, figure out a way to get it done.

Set a treadmill to its highest incline, head to a parkade, find some stairs, or pull a sled - all great substitutes for an actual hill.

If you're training for an obstacle race and aren't hitting the hills at least once a week, you're doing yourself a major disservice.

Getting the Most from Your Hill Training

Use these tips to stay injury-free and get the most from your hill training:

- *Slowing down is inevitable, so don't worry about maintaining your speed. Instead, focus on your cadence. Shorten your stride and keep those feet moving!*
- *Lean into the hill, but be sure not to bend at the waist. When we bend at the waist we push our hips and butt back. This alters our running form and decreases our running economy. Not only that, but bending at the hips will also compress our lungs, not allowing us to breathe full, deep breaths.*
- *Bend at the ankles, keeping your body as "plank-like" as possible - head, torso, hips, and feet aligned.*
- *When running downhill, continue to lean into the hill. Don't allow yourself to lean back and put on the breaks. This would result in hard, intense heel strikes and can cause some serious damage. Lean into the hill, maintain a comfortable pace, and trust that your feet will keep up.*

THE GASSER

We've been using this workout for a long time. It's fun, challenging, and great to do with a group of people.

Not only does this workout make us better obstacle racers, but it's also a true test of mental toughness. Transitioning quickly from pull-ups to a hill sprint is one thing, but having the guts and mental fortitude to hop right into a set of burpees at the top of the hill is something else entirely.

By the end of those burpees you will be gassed.

The goal of this workout is to push yourself by making your transition times as short as possible. Hop down from the pull-up bar and immediately start running. Once you reach the top of the hill, drop right into those burpees.

Doing so will build the confidence required to attack obstacles on the course.

Stopping to catch your breath before a tire flip or the monkey bars is a waste of time. And it could be the difference between qualifying for the World Championships and not.

"We all know that if you take 100m and walk up to that obstacle, you're going to be better off, but you just lost 30 seconds."

- Yancy Culp, Elite Obstacle Racing Coach

THE WORKOUT

- 5 Pull-ups/10 to 20-second Hill Sprint/10 Burpees
- Walk back down hill
- Repeat for 15 - 20 minutes

PROGRESSIONS

We've tried a variety of different reps for pull-ups and burpees, as well as different lengths of hills. I found that this set-up works quite well and wouldn't suggest changing either the 5 pull-ups or 10 burpees. If you are unable to do 5 pull-ups, do jumping pull-ups instead.

Doing the workout as described results in about one minute of intense activity.

The best way to progress this workout is to simply add time each week. Adding two minutes each week, combined with improved fitness, should allow for about an extra two sets each workout. A four-week progression could be set up like this:

Week 1:
- 5 pull-ups
- Hill sprint
- 10 burpees
- Walk back down hill
- Repeat for 14:00

Week 2:
- 5 pull-ups
- Hill sprint

- 10 burpees
- Walk back down hill
- Repeat for 16:00

Week 3:
- 5 pull-ups
- Hill sprint
- 10 burpees
- Walk back down hill
- Repeat for 18:00

Week 4:
- 5 pull-ups
- Hill sprint
- 10 burpees
- Walk back down hill
- Repeat for 20:00

LITVINOV

This workout is derived from an article elite-level strength and weightlifting coach Dan John wrote in 2006 called "The Litvinov Workout".

In his article, Dan outlines a training method inspired by 1983 World Champion hammer thrower Sergey Litvinov. It was said that in training, Litvinov would front squat 405 pounds (four plates per side!) for eight reps, rack the weight, then immediately run a 75 second 400m. Then he'd do it two more times.

There's no need for an obstacle racer to be able to front squat 405 pounds, but there is something magical about this style of training. By combining strength training and sprinting into one treacherous exercise athletes become, as Dan put it, "leaner, faster, and more muscular".

When done correctly, this workout is tough. Trying to run up a hill after an intense set of swings is one of the closest things I've found to running through the thick, deep mud you'll encounter on race day.

Your legs, and lungs, won't know what hit them.

- 30 KB Swings/20 to 40-second Hill Sprint
- Walk back down
- Rest 3 - 5 minutes between sets.
- Aim for 3 - 6 quality sets

PROGRESSIONS

We have a few options with this workout. We can progress the weight of the kettlebell for swings, the number of swings completed, the distance sprinted uphill, and/or the number of sets completed.

A four-week cycle altering the weight and repetitions of the kettlebell swing could look like this:

Week 1:
- 30 KB Swings - 16 kg
- 20s hill sprint
- Rest until recovered
- Repeat for 4 sets

Week 2:
- 40 KB Swings - 16 kg
- 20s hill sprint
- Rest until recovered
- Repeat for 4 sets

Week 3:
- 30 KB Swings - 24 kg
- 20s hill sprint
- Rest until recovered
- Repeat for 4 sets

Week 4:
- 40 KB Swings - 24 kg
- 20s hill sprint
- Rest until recovered
- Repeat for 4 sets

A four-week cycle altering the sprint could look like this:

Week 1:
- 30 KB Swings - 24 kg
- 20s hill sprint
- Rest until recovered
- Repeat for 4 sets

Week 2:
- 30 KB Swings - 24 kg
- 25s hill sprint
- Rest until recovered
- Repeat for 4 sets

Week 3:
- 30 KB Swings - 24 kg
- 30s hill sprint
- Rest until recovered
- Repeat for 4 sets

Week 4:
- 30 KB Swings - 24 kg
- 35s hill sprint
- Rest until recovered
- Repeat for 4 sets

A four-week cycle altering the number of sets could look like this:

Week 1:
- 30 KB Swings - 24 kg
- 20s hill sprint
- Rest until recovered
- Repeat for 3 sets

Week 2:
- 30 KB Swings - 24 kg
- 20s hill sprint
- Rest until recovered
- Repeat for 4 sets

Week 3:
- 30 KB Swings - 24 kg
- 20s hill sprint
- Rest until recovered
- Repeat for 5 sets

Week 4:
- 30 KB Swings - 24 kg
- 20s hill sprint
- Rest until recovered
- Repeat for 6 sets

1 KM Hill Repeats

Hill sprints are great, but we also need to spend some real time on the hills as well. We typically reserve this workout for later in the season, after we've spent a few weeks getting ready for the longer duration.

Most running coaches will disagree with the idea of running at tempo pace on hills. Keep in mind, though, that we are training for races on hills and not on flat, paved roads.

If we want to be able to race fast on hills, we need to occasionally train fast on hills.

THE WORKOUT

- Find a hill or hilly area that will allow for you to run one kilometer (can be up and down hill)
- Run the 1 km course at a tempo pace (85-90% Max Heart Rate)
- Do two sets of exercises for your weak areas (push-ups, flutter kicks, pull-ups, farmer walks, etc.) while recovering from run
- Walk around until heart rate has dropped to 60-65% Max Heart Rate
    - If you don't have access to a heart rate monitor, use the "Talk Test" - rest and recover until you can comfortably hold a conversation
- Repeat for 3 - 8 sets (based on length of upcoming race)

PROGRESSIONS

There are a few ways to gradually make this workout more difficult. You could use a steeper hill each week, but that may be unrealistic. Your best options are to either add sets each week, and/or add repetitions or choose more difficult exercises between 1km runs.

For example, a four-week cycle of this workout, adding sets each week, could look like this:

Week 1:
- Run 1km course
- 15 Push-ups
- 10-meter Farmer Walk
- Rest until recovered
- Repeat for 3 sets

48

Week 2:
- Run 1km course
- 15 Push-ups
- 10-meter Farmer Walk
- Rest until recovered
- Repeat for 4 sets

Week 3:
- Run 1km course
- 15 Push-ups
- 10-meter Farmer Walk
- Rest until recovered
- Repeat for 5 sets

Week 4:
- Run 1km course
- 15 Push-ups
- 10-meter Farmer Walk
- Rest until recovered
- Repeat for 6 sets

Another four-week cycle, where we instead change our exercises between 1km runs, could look like this:

Week 1:
- Run 1km course
- 15 Push-ups
- 10-meter Farmer Walk
- Rest until recovered
- Repeat for 4 sets

Week 2:
- Run 1km course
- 20 Push-ups
- 15-meter Farmer Walk
- Rest until recovered
- Repeat for 4 sets

Week 3:
- Run 1km course
- 25 Push-ups
- 20-meter Farmer Walk
- Rest until recovered
- Repeat for 4 sets

Week 4:
- Run 1km course
- 30 Push-ups
- 25-meter Farmer Walk
- Rest until recovered
- Repeat for 4 sets

Interval Workouts

Our interval workouts are not like what you'll find at your local gym. These are not "HIIT Class" or "Tabata Burn" sessions. The goal of these workouts isn't to boost our metabolism, tighten and tone, or sweat buckets.

The goal is to become a better athlete.

Our intervals are about going hard, getting fast, and pushing ourselves. More than anything, these workouts are built to increase our speed and mental toughness.

Five pull-ups are easy, but are you mentally tough enough to jump right into a set after a 400m sprint?

Because we aren't logging many miles in our training, we utilize intervals such as these to become better overall runners.

"Interval training has been a part of all solid training plans for decades. It's a proven way to increase your running efficiency and VO2 max, with performance benefits far surpassing long slow distance (LSD) and lactate threshold (LT) running."

- Pete Hitzeman, Coach & Assistant Editor, Breaking Muscle

These workouts may not seem like much on paper, but once you try them with the proper intensity you'll find they can be *gut wrenching*.

We aim for negative splits during these workouts (i.e. we try to go faster/further on each interval).

While we may set a certain number of repetitions or time allotment at the beginning of the training session, we stop our workouts "when we're done".

If our times start to slow too much, or we can't run as far during the allotted time, we pack it in and call it a day.

This is done for a couple of reasons.

First, it helps us ensure we don't go too hard too fast during our workout - we aren't trying to set any world records during the first few intervals of our session. Second, it's a way of self regulating.

If we continue to train after we've peaked, we're only going to end up digging ourselves too deep a hole.

We'll be overworked, unable to recover, and this will negatively affect our next week (or longer) of workouts.

For example, if we are doing our OCR Speed Work workout and an athlete's times look like this:

Set 1 - 1:30
Set 2 - 1:27
Set 3 - 1:20
Set 4 - 1:22
Set 5 - 1:35

It becomes obvious that this athlete pushed themselves too hard on their third set. We would abruptly end that athlete's workout after the fifth set, even if they were scheduled for 8 sets that day.

You can't improve your speed if you can no longer run fast.

We try to end these workouts feeling good. We want to feel fast, but not beat up.

OCR Speed Work

Everyone loves 400m repeats!

...well, maybe not everyone. But they're an important part of any runner's repertoire nonetheless.

These repeats should be run near (ideally just above) your anaerobic threshold pace, or your "fastest maintainable speed".

"Physiologically, threshold training teaches muscle cells to use more Oxygen–less lactate is produced. Your body also becomes better at clearing lactate: race-day red line speed rises."

- Jack Daniels, Elite Running Coach and Exercise Physiologist

If we were training for a 5k, half-marathon, or other typical road race, simply doing 400m repeats would be enough. For obstacle course racing, however, we need to add a bit more. That's why we add pull-ups, either on a bar, rings, tree branch, ropes, or a towel, immediately after our 400m.

Like our "**Gasser**" workout in the Hill Workout section, this provides another opportunity to work on our mental toughness and decrease our obstacle transition times. Being able to confidently attack an obstacle, or in this case - a set of pull-ups, while your whole body is burning is a very useful skill for OCR.

This one is simple, but effective. We used it during our Speed and Endurance sessions on an almost weekly basis.

THE WORKOUT

- Run 400m
- Immediately do 5 - 10 pull-ups
- Rest 1:30 - 2:00 between sets
- Repeat for 4 - 10 sets

PROGRESSIONS

The best way to progress this workout is to start with longer (2:00 rest periods) and gradually decrease them. If you were planning on doing this workout once a week for four weeks, for example, you could set it up like this:

Week 1:
- 400m run
- 5 pull-ups
- 2:00 rest
- Repeat for 6 sets

Week 2:
- 400m run
- 5 pull-ups
- 1:50 rest
- Repeat for 6 sets

Week 3:
- 400m run
- 5 pull-ups
- 1:40 rest
- Repeat for 6 sets

Week 4:
- 400m run

- 5 pull-ups
- 1:30 rest
- Repeat for 6 sets

After this four week cycle you could start over with 2:00 rest periods, but increase the number of pull-ups. For example:

Week 1:
- 400m run
- 7 pull-ups
- 2:00 rest
- Repeat for 6 sets

Week 2:
- 400m run
- 7 pull-ups
- 1:50 rest
- Repeat for 6 sets

Week 3:
- 400m run
- 7 pull-ups
- 1:40 rest
- Repeat for 6 sets

Week 4:
- 400m run
- 7 pull-ups
- 1:30 rest
- Repeat for 6 sets

Another way to cycle this workout would be to simply add sets each workout. For example:

Week 1:
- 400m run
- 5 pull-ups
- 2:00 rest
- Repeat for 5 sets

Week 2:
- 400m run
- 5 pull-ups
- 2:00 rest
- Repeat for 6 sets

Week 3:
- 400m run
- 5 pull-ups
- 2:00 rest
- Repeat for 7 sets

Week 4:
- 400m run
- 5 pull-ups
- 2:00 rest
- Repeat for 8 sets

SANDBAGS AND SPEED

Heavy carries are a key part of obstacle racing.

Carrying something heavy, *up hill*, for 200 - 400 meters is a completely different stress on the body than running. Obstacles like these are the big equalizer of obstacle course racing – they slow the smaller, speedier athletes down, while they give the bigger, stronger ones a chance to catch up.

Buckets and sandbags simply change the game.

The goal of this workout is to carry a sandbag for 200m at a relatively quick pace, then drop it and start running.

Don't set it down nicely, check to make sure your shoes are tied, take a few deep breaths and start jogging away - **drop it and run**.

Training the Transition

You should be seeing a theme here.

I believe that training for the transition between running and obstacles is very important. We need to put our mind and body through this process as much as possible during our training to prevent us from slowing down on race day.

THE WORKOUT

- 200m sandbag carry
- Drop sandbag and sprint 400m
- Recover until heart rate has dropped to 60-65% Max Heart Rate
    - If you don't have access to a heart rate monitor, use the "Talk Test" - rest and recover until you can comfortably hold a conversation
- Repeat for 4 - 10 sets

PROGRESSIONS

The best way to progress with this workout is by adding sets each week. For example, a four-week progression could look like this:

Week 1:
- 200m sandbag carry - 60 lbs.
- 400m run
- Rest until recovered
- Repeat for 4 sets

Week 2:
- 200m sandbag carry - 60 lbs.
- 400m run
- Rest until recovered
- Repeat for 5 sets

Week 3:
- 200m sandbag carry - 60 lbs.
- 400m run
- Rest until recovered
- Repeat for 6 sets

Week 4:
- 200m sandbag carry - 60 lbs.
- 400m run
- Rest until recovered
- Repeat for 7 sets

Another other option would be to use a slightly heavier sandbag with each workout. For example:

Week 1:
- 200m sandbag carry - 30 lbs.
- 400m run
- Rest until recovered
- Repeat for 6 sets

Week 2:
- 200m sandbag carry - 40 lbs.
- 400m run
- Rest until recovered
- Repeat for 6 sets

Week 3:
- 200m sandbag carry - 50 lbs.
- 400m run
- Rest until recovered
- Repeat for 6 sets

Week 4:
- 200m sandbag carry - 60 lbs.
- 400m run
- Rest until recovered
- Repeat for 6 sets

3 ON/3 OFF

Not all our interval workouts consist of 400m repeats. This one is instead based off time instead of distance.

Rather than running 400m and trying to complete each set faster than before, this workout is based on trying to run a bit further with each interval.

You'll need a watch or timer set to go off every three minutes, and a path or trail approximately 800 – 1,200 meters long. The path can be a loop, or "there and back" (run 400-600m out, then run back to starting point).

The idea is to run the first set at about 85% effort and increase your effort with each set. Begin at the starting line and run until your 3:00 timer goes off. Mark your spot on the path or trail and walk back to the starting line. Recover until your 3:00 rest period is up, then try to run farther during the next interval.

This is a tough workout, but it's a lot of fun trying to beat yourself during those last couple of intervals.

THE WORKOUT

- Begin at the start line, run as far as possible during your 3:00, starting with about 85% effort
- After 3:00, stop and mark where you ended. 3:00 rest period starts immediately after 3:00 run ends
- Walk back to the start line and begin again once your 3:00 rest period is up
- Try to get a bit further than previous mark on your next interval
- Repeat for 5 rounds of 3:00 on/3:00 off (total of 30:00 workout) trying to beat previous distance each round.
- On the fifth and final round, feel free to push as hard as possible

PROGRESSIONS

There isn't much we can do to progress this workout besides pushing ourselves a bit harder and trying to beat our farthest distance during the fifth and final set of each workout.

It is essentially a "self-progressing" workout.

AMRAP Workouts

I don't do Crossfit. I've never even stepped inside a Crossfit Box.

I have, however, been doing AMRAP (As Many Rounds as Possible) workouts long before there was a fancy name for them.

It's great that so many people are now on the AMRAP bandwagon. However, I think inappropriate movements, exercises, and loads are chosen too often.

Doing Olympic or power lifts as quickly as possible while fatigued may seem fun, but the risk far outweighs the reward in my opinion.

Especially once the load begins to creep close to an athlete's one rep max.

Trying to do very technical lifts as fast as possible with heavy weights just doesn't seem like a great idea to me.

Our AMRAP and "For Time" (next section) workouts utilize running, bodyweight movements, relatively light loads, and are done over longer periods of time than what you'd see elsewhere.

It's not that we *don't* do AMRAPs for ten or twenty minutes, but we are very careful about programming them.

AMRAP workouts are fun, and great ways to measure progress. Getting more rounds in shows that you are progressing and your training is working.

Even if it's just an extra rep or half a round, these small wins can be very motivating.

The three AMRAP workouts listed below are all done for 45:00. We do this for several reasons, including:

1. It forces us to work on pacing.
2. The slower pace ensures our athletes are not rushing through the workout with sloppy form thus risking injury.
3. The longer workout makes it more mentally challenging, forcing us to practice focus and grit.
4. Going much longer than 45:00 would start to have negative hormonal repercussions.

100M RUN/5 BURPEES

This workout may seem boring on paper, but when done on a hot, summer day with a group of friends, it can be a ton of fun.

The trick to this workout, as you'll find, is to pace yourself. I've seen people start out real strong, finishing sets in under 30 seconds, only to gas out and finish the workout at a snail's pace. Don't do this.

Remember, one of the goals of these workouts is to improve pacing.

Aim for your 5k pace and you'll do great. Feel free to go hard during the last 5 minutes to emulate that final push at the end of a race. Those final five minutes can be the difference between leaving the venue with your Spartan Coin and leaving empty handed.

The best place to do this workout is a football or soccer field where the goal posts roughly mark 100 meters.

THE WORKOUT

- Starting at one set of goalposts, run (~5K pace) to the goalposts on the other side of the field
- Drop and do 5 burpees
- Repeat for as many rounds as possible in 45:00

PROGRESSIONS

I believe the best way to incorporate this workout is to keep it as is and complete it once per month. If you wanted to focus on this workout for a few weeks, however, you could progress the length of time. For example, a four-week progression could look like this:

Week 1:
- 100m run
- 5 burpees
- Repeat for 30:00

Week 2:
- 100m run
- 5 burpees
- Repeat for 35:00

Week 3:
- 100m run
- 5 burpees
- Repeat for 40:00

Week 4:
- 100m run
- 5 burpees
- Repeat for 45:00

PLAYGROUND OBSTACLE COURSE

This is the first Obstacle Course Racing workout we ever programmed. And we've stuck with it ever since. It provides everything you need to succeed in OCR.

I believe that if you can find a good playground, you can become a good obstacle racer.

Look for things like monkey bars, balance beams, bouldering walls, benches, walls to climb and jump over, and tobogganing hills. Also, don't be afraid to bring your own obstacles. We use buckets, salt bags, sand bags, broom handles for spear throws, cinder blocks, climbing ropes, slacklines, and more.

The goal of this workout is really to get some endurance work in while practicing transitioning from running, to obstacle, and back to running again. Work on your grit and determination, don't stop to catch your breath or pat yourself on the back - see how fast you can transition.

Minutes get wasted every race from the pre/post obstacle "pep talk" we give to ourselves. Make quick, seamless transitioning a habit in practice and you'll do the same during the race.

THE WORKOUT

- Head to a local playground and set up an obstacle course utilizing things like buckets, salt bags, monkey bars, rock walls, balance beams, parallel bars. Get creative!
- Aim for 5 - 10 obstacles over a 500m - 1km course
- Get through the course as many times as possible in 45:00

PROGRESSIONS

We do two different variations of this workout. Sometimes we run through the course, stopping and completing each obstacle along the way. Other times we will complete an obstacle, then run an entire lap around the course before stopping at the next obstacle.

Which option you should choose depends on what you want to focus on.

If you need to spend more time learning to complete the obstacles, then stop at each obstacle along the way. On the other hand, if you need to focus more on your running, try running a full lap between obstacles.

As far as structured progressions go, a great option is to add an obstacle each week.

A sample four-week progression could look like this:

Week 1:
- 800m course with 5 obstacles
- Complete as many laps as possible in 45:00

Week 2:
- 800m course with 6 obstacles
- Complete as many laps as possible in 45:00

Week 3:
- 800m course with 7 obstacles
- Complete as many laps as possible in 45:00

Week 4:
- 800m course with 8 obstacles
- Complete as many laps as possible in 45:00

Burpees/Loaded Carries

This one isn't the most popular with our athletes because when done right, it's quite challenging.

It's not uncommon for our athletes to do over 300 burpees and over 1km of loaded carries in just 45:00.

The idea is to get a ton of volume in, while trying to maintain a consistent pace throughout. We don't want our last rounds taking much longer than our first few, if at all.

This workout is a great opportunity to work on pacing.

If you start out going too hard you will crash and burn before the 45:00 are up. If you go too slow, however, you won't get nearly as effective a training session.

This is what pacing is all about - learning how hard we can push ourselves without blowing up.

THE WORKOUT

- Complete 30 Burpees
- Immediately grab a weight implement (sandbag, kettlebell, bucket, we like to fireman carry each other as well) and carry it for 50 - 200 meters
- Complete as many rounds as possible in 45:00

PROGRESSIONS

With this workout, you can change either the weight or type of object for the loaded carries, as well as the distance. Here are a couple of options.

Changing weight of loaded carry:

Week 1:
- 30 Burpees
- 100m 40 lbs Bucket carry
- Repeat for 45:00

Week 2:
- 30 Burpees
- 100m 50 lbs Bucket carry
- Repeat for 45:00

Week 3:
- 30 Burpees
- 100m 60 lbs Bucket carry
- Repeat for 45:00

Week 4:
- 30 Burpees
- 100m 70 lbs Bucket carry

- Repeat for 45:00

Changing distance of loaded carry:

Week 1:
- 30 Burpees
- 50m 50 lbs Bucket carry
- Repeat for 45:00

Week 2:
- 30 Burpees
- 100m 50 lbs Bucket carry
- Repeat for 45:00

Week 3:
- 30 Burpees
- 150m 50 lbs Bucket carry
- Repeat for 45:00

Week 4:
- 30 Burpees
- 200m 50 lbs Bucket carry
- Repeat for 45:00

For either of these progressions the goal should be to aim for the same number of rounds each week, even though the carries get progressively more difficult.

Another option is to progress the burpees over time. A four-week progression could look something like this:

Week 1:
- 8 Burpees
- 200m 50 lbs Bucket carry

- Repeat for 45:00

Week 2:
- 16 Burpees
- 200m 50 lbs Bucket carry
- Repeat for 45:00

Week 3:
- 24 Burpees
- 200m 50 lbs Bucket carry
- Repeat for 45:00

Week 4:
- 30 Burpees
- 200m 50 lbs Bucket carry
- Repeat for 45:00

For Time Workouts

Sometimes you just need to go hard and fast.

That's where these workouts come in. These are the workouts where we really let our athletes push themselves and see what they're made of.

Like our AMRAP workouts, we do not use super heavy weights or complex movements that are difficult to execute while fatigued. We stick to the basics - burpees, squats, push-ups, loaded carries, and focus on intensity. Doing anything else is dangerous.

While pacing is important during these sessions, we don't want to hit a wall halfway through but we also want to make sure we aren't holding back.

PUSH PRESS/ZERCHER SQUAT/BURPEE REVERSE LADDER

As someone with more of a strength than endurance background, this is one of my favorite workouts; *especially when done with a sandbag.*

Not only do sandbags provide a unique challenge as the unstable weight moves around as you lift it, but it's also fun slamming it to the ground when you're done!

We've done several variations of this workout in the past, but this is one of our favorites. With push-presses, Zercher squats, and burpees all rolled into one, it's the definition of "full-body workout".

The reverse ladder format of this workout (starting with high reps and decreasing the number with every round) allow for us to get in a lot of volume while maintaining momentum.

If we were to do all 110 reps of each exercise as simply 10 rounds of 11, not only would the workout be boring, but we would likely slow down significantly. With the reverse ladder, each set gets easier and so we are more likely to attack it with the required intensity.

THE WORKOUT

- Using a sandbag, rock, or similar implement, complete 20 Push Presses, 20 Zercher Squats, and 20 Burpees
- Immediately after the burpees, do 18 of each exercise
- Carry on, removing 2 reps from each exercise each round, until down to zero
- You will end up doing 10 sets of the following reps:
  - 20, 18, 16, 14, 12, 10, 8, 6, 4, 2
- Complete this workout as fast as possible without resting between exercises

PROGRESSIONS

The best way to progress this workout is by cycling the weight. For example, a four-week progression could look like this:

Week 1:
- Complete workout with 40 lbs sandbag

Week 2:
- Complete workout with 50 lbs sandbag

Week 3:
- Complete workout with 60 lbs sandbag

Week 4:
- Complete workout with 70 lbs sandbag

Simply trying to beat your time each week is another form of progression with this workout.

Hill Sandwich

The closest we've ever come to having athletes collapse during a workout was during the Hill Sandwich. But we'll just blame that on the heat.

This is a tough one, and it's always interesting to see where each athlete struggles the most. It is a great indicator of their weaknesses and what we should be working on in our training.

Fifty consecutive pull-ups (not one continuous set, but broken up into as many smaller sets as needed) is a fantastic test of grip strength endurance. Completing 100 consecutive push-ups tests our pushing strength and abdominal endurance. Follow that up with 150 squats, and running up and down a hill ten times, and you'll see what kind of shape your legs are in.

Doing it all twice? That's where we see what we're really made of.

Completing this workout will require you to find a small hill (should be able to run up and down the hill in about 10-20 seconds) and somewhere to do pull-ups (monkey bars, rings, tree branch, swing set, etc.).

THE WORKOUT

- Run up and down hill 10 times
    - 50 pull-ups
    - 100 push-ups
    - 150 squats
- Run up and down hill 10 times
    - 50 pull-ups
    - 100 push-ups
    - 150 squats
- Run up and down hill 10 times
- Complete this workout as fast as possible

Note: *The strength exercises are to be done consecutively; i.e. complete all 50 pull-ups before moving on to push-ups, complete all 100 push-ups before moving on to squats, complete all 150 squats before moving on to hills. Feel free to break them up into as many sets as possible (e.g. 10 sets of 5 pull-ups), but remember that the idea is to finish this workout as quickly as possible.*

PROGRESSIONS

The prescribed number of repetitions for each strength exercise may be a bit much for some. If this is the case, feel free to progress to the full workout over time. For example, a four-week progression could look like this:

Week 1:
- Run up and down hill 10 times
    - 20 pull-ups
    - 40 push-ups
    - 60 squats

- Repeat
- Run up and down hill 10 times

Week 2:
- Run up and down hill 10 times
    - 30 pull-ups
    - 60 push-ups
    - 90 squats
- Repeat
- Run up and down hill 10 times

Week 3:
- Run up and down hill 10 times
    - 40 pull-ups
    - 80 push-ups
    - 120 squats
- Repeat
- Run up and down hill 10 times

Week 4:
- Run up and down hill 10 times
    - 50 pull-ups
    - 100 push-ups
    - 150 squats
- Repeat
- Run up and down hill 10 times

Run/Carry/20's

This workout provides a nice combination of running, loaded carries, and bodyweight movements. It can be a lot of fun racing beside your friends and teammates while completing this workout.

As this workout is done for time and is filled with easy to-do movements, it's one of the few workouts where we'll try to really go hard and compete. That added sense of urgency helps to keep us going even after we're exhausted; a skill we need to develop if we want to be successful on race day.

The best place to do this workout is at a trail or park.

You'll need a weight of some sort (bucket, sandbag, heavy kettlebell, etc.) and something to mark out points at 50m and 400m away. When running your 800m, run to the 400m marker and back. When doing the loaded carries, you'll use the 50m marker.

THE WORKOUT

- Bring a sandbag/bucket/etc. to a park
- Set a marker 400m out, and one 50m out
- Do the following for 4 rounds, as fast as possible:
    - 800m run (to the 400m marker and back)
    - Carry weight (sandbag, bucket, kettlebell, or other) to 50m marker
    - 20 bodyweight squats
    - Carry weight back to starting point
    - 20 push-ups
    - Carry weight back to 50m marker
    - 20 Lunges (10 each leg)
    - Carry weight back to starting point
    - 20 Hollow Rocks

PROGRESSIONS

Rather than trying to make this workout progressively more difficult, I would recommend switching up the bodyweight movements to keep things fresh. While I prefer the squats, push-ups, lunges, and hollow rocks, other good options would be:

- Pull-ups
- V-Sits
- Reverse Lunges
- Jump squats
- Feet-elevated push-ups
- Swings, snatches, or goblet squats (if using a kettlebell for loaded carry)

Putting It All Together

At the beginning of this book, we mentioned how our workouts are short, intense, fun, and effective.

If you follow the workouts as describe, I'm confident you'll agree they fit these criteria.

To reach your true potential, however, or to become good enough to race Elite or qualify for the World Championships, it's not as simple as just picking a random workout for the day.

To be the best we can be, we need to put a bit more thought into it than that.

We've listed four different types of workouts, and provided three workouts for each, for a total of 12 fun and effective training sessions. We've also discussed ways to progress each of those twelve workouts over the course of four weeks.

The best way to incorporate these workouts into your training is to focus on a select few each month and follow the progressions.

Find some friends to train with, add in a few easy trail-runs each week, and you're ready to rock!

The following is a list of sample programs using these workouts based on two, three, or four training sessions per week.

SAMPLE PROGRAMS

TWO SESSIONS PER WEEK

Tuesdays: Litvinov

Week 1:
- 30 KB Swings - 24 kg
- 20s hill sprint
- Rest until recovered
- Repeat for 3 sets

Week 2:
- 30 KB Swings - 24 kg
- 20s hill sprint
- Rest until recovered
- Repeat for 4 sets

Week 3:
- 30 KB Swings - 24 kg
- 20s hill sprint
- Rest until recovered
- Repeat for 5 sets

Week 4:
- 30 KB Swings - 24 kg
- 20s hill sprint
- Rest until recovered
- Repeat for 6 sets

Thursdays: 100m Run/5 Burpees

Week 1:
- 100m run
- 5 burpees
- Repeat for 30:00

Week 2:
- 100m run
- 5 burpees
- Repeat for 35:00

Week 3:
- 100m run
- 5 burpees
- Repeat for 40:00

Week 4:
- 100m run
- 5 burpees
- Repeat for 45:00

Mondays: The Gasser

Week 1:
- 5 pull-ups
- Hill sprint
- 10 burpees
- Walk back down hill
- Repeat for 14:00

Week 2:
- 5 pull-ups
- Hill sprint
- 10 burpees
- Walk back down hill
- Repeat for 16:00

Week 3:
- 5 pull-ups
- Hill sprint
- 10 burpees
- Walk back down hill
- Repeat for 18:00

Week 4:
- 5 pull-ups
- Hill sprint
- 10 burpees
- Walk back down hill
- Repeat for 20:00

Wednesdays: Burpees/Loaded Carries

Week 1:
- 30 Burpees
- 100m 40 lbs Bucket carry
- Repeat for 45:00

Week 2:
- 30 Burpees
- 100m 50 lbs Bucket carry
- Repeat for 45:00

Week 3:
- 30 Burpees
- 100m 60 lbs Bucket carry
- Repeat for 45:00

Week 4:
- 30 Burpees
- 100m 70 lbs Bucket carry
- Repeat for 45:00

Fridays: Push Press/Zercher Squat/Burpee Reverse Ladder

Week 1:
- Complete workout with 40 lbs sandbag

Week 2:
- Complete workout with 50 lbs sandbag

Week 3:
- Complete workout with 60 lbs sandbag

Week 4:
- Complete workout with 70 lbs sandbag

Four Sessions Per Week

Tuesdays: OCR Speed Work

Week 1:
- 400m run
- 5 pull-ups
- 2:00 rest
- Repeat for 5 sets

Week 2:
- 400m run
- 5 pull-ups
- 1:50 rest
- Repeat for 5 sets

Week 3:
- 400m run
- 5 pull-ups
- 1:40 rest
- Repeat for 5 sets

Week 4:
- 400m run
- 5 pull-ups
- 1:30 rest
- Repeat for 5 sets

Thursdays: Hill Sandwich

Week 1:
- Run up and down hill 10 times
  - 20 pull-ups
  - 40 push-ups
  - 60 squats
- Repeat
- Run up and down hill 10 times

Week 2:
- Run up and down hill 10 times
  - 30 pull-ups
  - 60 push-ups
  - 90 squats
- Repeat
- Run up and down hill 10 times

Week 3:
- Run up and down hill 10 times
  - 40 pull-ups
  - 80 push-ups
  - 120 squats
- Repeat
- Run up and down hill 10 times

Week 4:
- Run up and down hill 10 times
  - 50 pull-ups
  - 100 push-ups
  - 150 squats
- Repeat
- Run up and down hill 10 times

Saturdays: 1 Km Hill Repeats

Week 1:
- Run 1km course
- 15 Push-ups
- 10m Farmer Walk
- Rest until recovered
- Repeat for 3 sets

Week 2:
- Run 1km course
- 15 Push-ups
- 10m Farmer Walk
- Rest until recovered
- Repeat for 4 sets

Week 3:
- Run 1km course
- 15 Push-ups
- 10m Farmer Walk
- Rest until recovered
- Repeat for 5 sets

Week 4:
- Run 1km course
- 15 Push-ups
- 10m Farmer Walk
- Rest until recovered
- Repeat for 6 sets

Sundays: Playground Obstacle Course

Note: *After Saturday's hill repeats, it's a good idea to view this workout as a recovery run with obstacle practice thrown in the middle. Stay with a light jog, keeping your heart rate low and practice your technique.*

While the workout states "Complete as many laps as possible in 45:00", don't push yourself too hard just to get more laps in (make sure you stay aerobic).

Week 1:
- 800m course with 5 obstacles
- Complete as many laps as possible in 45:00

Week 2:
- 800m course with 6 obstacles
- Complete as many laps as possible in 45:00

Week 3:
- 800m course with 7 obstacles
- Complete as many laps as possible in 45:00

Week 4:
- 800m course with 8 obstacles
- Complete as many laps as possible in 45:00

THE POWER OF A TEAM

If you follow the laid-out programs in this book you *will* become a better obstacle racer. The true secret to our success, however, is that we support and push each other as a team.

Through our Private Facebook Group and workout tracking software, our athletes from across Canada can keep in touch and see how their training is going relative to their teammates.

We know who trained that day and who didn't. We can see how fast our teammates finished a workout or how much weight they used. We congratulate each other when we hit a personal best and help each other through the inevitable setbacks.

It is because of this team environment that over 70% of our athletes qualified for the Obstacle Course Racing World Championships last year.

We're always looking to add to our team. It doesn't matter to us how fast or strong you are. All we look for is a hard working, positive team player.

If you're interested in professional workout programming and the support of a strong team environment, head to TrainWithConviction.com and check us out. We'd love to hear from you.

About The Author

Riley Nadoroznick is an experienced nutrition, strength, and conditioning coach with an unmatched passion for helping people become happier and healthier.

A former collegiate wrestler and current Spartan Race Elite athlete, Riley combines his multiple certifications with twenty plus years of training experience to help others reach their health and fitness goals.

As a lifelong student of strength, conditioning, and nutrition, Riley is devoted to improving his knowledge through countless hours of reading and studying the latest health and fitness information.

In his free time, Riley enjoys spending time with his wife and kids, and can often be found stretching on the floor with a book in his hands.

Pick-up the #1 Bestseller on Amazon.

Made in the USA
Columbia, SC
27 December 2019

85877070R00067